DISSERTATIONS ON ANGLO-IRISH DRAMA

Dissertations on Anglo-Irish Drama

A Bibliography of Studies 1870–1970

E. H. Mikhail

Professor of English Literature
University of Lethbridge, Canada

ROWMAN AND LITTLEFIELD
TOTOWA, NEW JERSEY

First published in the United States 1973
by Rowman and Littlefield, Totowa, N.J.

First published in the United Kingdom 1973 by
The Macmillan Press Ltd

Library of Congress Cataloging in Publication Data

Mikhail, E   H
    Dissertations on Anglo-Irish drama.

    1.   English drama—Irish authors—History and
criticism—Bibliography.   2.   Dissertations,
Academic—Bibliography.   I.   Title.
Z2039.D7M54   016.822'009   73—6967
ISBN 0 - 87471 - 203 - 3

Printed in Great Britain

To ISABELLE

CONTENTS

PREFACE

Studies in Anglo-Irish Drama—as this bibliography itself demonstrates—are assuming greater proportions with each passing year. The result is an unusually large output of dissertations, of which only a limited number have yet been published in their entirety. This volume, the first bibliography ever to appear in print devoted completely to dissertations on Anglo-Irish Drama, lists more than 500 dissertations on 24 dramatists completed between 1870 and 1970 at a large number of universities in Great Britain, Ireland, the United States, Germany, France, and Canada. In addition to the author's name, complete title and sub-title of the dissertation, and the university to which it was submitted, the bibliographic listing is supplemented by two indexes intended to enhance its utility: one by author, and the other by institution.

An authoritative index to dissertations does not exist. The *Index to Theses Accepted for Higher Degrees in the Universities of Great Britain and Ireland* restricts itself to British universities and starts only from 1950. *American Doctoral Dissertations*, again, confines itself to American universities and has no playwright index; the reader has to go through the whole section dealing with 'English Literature' in order to find what he is looking for. The same limitation applies to Gisela Schwanbeck's *Bibliographie der deutschsprachigen Hochschulschriften zur Theaterwissenschaft von 1885 bis 1952* and Hans Jurgen Rojek's *Bibliographie der deutschsprachigen Hochschulschriften zur Theaterwissenschaft von 1953 bis 1960*. *Dissertation Abstracts* is by no means a complete record of recent doctoral scholarship, and one has to spend a long time searching through volumes of abstracts. Lawrence McNamee's *Dissertations in English and American Literature; Theses Accepted by American, British and German Univer-*

sities is more comprehensive in scope, but unsatisfactory in arrangement. It lists both Synge and Yeats, for example, under 'Nineteenth Century Drama'. Frederic M. Litto's *American Dissertations on the Drama and The Theatre: A Bibliography* is well arranged but incomplete in content; it lists only five dissertations on Synge, whereas the number is by far larger than that.

This is not, in any way, to derogate from the existing bibliographies. It is merely to draw attention to the difficulty that confronts the researcher in this field, as well as to the need at last for a comprehensive and definitive bibliography of research in Anglo-Irish Drama from 1870 to 1970. This bibliography was undertaken in the hope of satisfying this need. In addition to serving as a reference work for experienced scholars, this bibliography points up gaps in scholarship and can eliminate the duplication of dissertation subjects by doctoral candidates.

My gratitude must reach out to many more than I can name in these pages. Particular acknowledgement of indebtedness must include thanks to the staffs of almost two hundred university libraries, who were always helpful and gracious about answering hundreds of requests for detailed information. Miss Bea Ramtej has undertaken the difficult task of preparing the final typescript.

E. H. MIKHAIL

Lethbridge, Canada
March 1973

1 GENERAL

Abood, Edward F., 'The Reception of the Abbey Theater in America, 1911-14', Ph.D., University of Chicago, 1963.

Allt, G. D. P., 'The Anglo-Irish Literary Movement in Relation to Its Antecedents', Ph.D., Cambridge University, 1952.

Bergholz, Harry, 'Die Neugestaltung Des Modernen Englischen Theaterwesens und Ihre Bedeutung Für Den Spielplan', Ph.D., Berlin University, 1933.

Bernardbehan, Brother Merrill, 'Anglo-Irish Literature', M.A., University of Montreal, 1939.

Berrow, J. H., 'A Study of the Background Treatment and Presentation of Irish Character in British Plays from the Late 19th Century to the Present Day', M.A., University of Wales, Swansea, 1966.

Byars, John Arthur, 'The Heroic in the Irish Legendary Dramas of W. B. Yeats, Lady Gregory, and J. M. Synge, 1903-1910', Ph.D., University of North Carolina, 1963.

Cole, A. S., 'Stagecraft in the Modern Dublin Theatre', Ph.D., Trinity College Dublin, 1953.

Coleman, Sr Anne G., 'Social and Political Satire in Irish Drama', Ph.D., University of Fordham, 1954.

Cooper, Mabel, 'The Irish Theatre: Its History and Its Dramatists', M.A., University of Manitoba, 1931.

1

General

Cotter, Eileen M., 'The Deirdre Theme in Anglo-Irish Literature', Ph.D., University of California, Los Angeles, 1967.

Holzapfel, R. P., 'A Survey of Irish Literary Periodicals from 1900 to the Present Day', M.Litt., Trinity College Dublin, 1963.

Kelson, John Hofstad, 'Nationalism in the Theater: The Ole Bull Theater in Norway and the Abbey Theater in Ireland: A Comparative Study', Ph.D., University of Kansas, 1964.

Lyman, Kenneth C., 'Critical Reaction to Irish Drama on the New York Stage, 1900-1958', Ph.D., University of Wisconsin, 1960.

Mcguire, James Brady, 'Realism in Irish Drama', Ph.D., Trinity College Dublin, 1954.

McHenry, Margaret, 'The Ulster Theatre in Ireland', Ph.D., University of Pennsylvania, 1931.

Madden, Regina D., 'The Literary Criticism of the Irish Renaissance', Ph.D., University of Boston, 1938.

Miller, Marcia S. K., 'The Deirdre Legend in English Literature', Ph.D., University of Pennsylvania, 1950.

O'Neill, Michael J., 'The Diaries of a Dublin Playgoer as a Mirror of the Irish Literary Revival', Ph.D., National University, Dublin, 1952.

Oppren, Genevieve L., 'The Irish Players in America', M.A., University of Washington, 1943.

Peteler, Patricia M., 'The Social and Symbolic Drama of the English-Language Theatre, 1929-1949', Ph.D., University of Utah, 1961.

Randall, Ethel Claire, 'The Celtic Movement; The Awakening of the Fire', M.A., University of Chicago, 1906.

General

Saddlemyer, E. Ann, 'A Study of the Dramatic Theory Developed by the Founders of the Irish Literary Theatre and the Attempt to Apply This Theory in the Abbey Theatre, with Particular Reference to the Achievement of the Major Figures during the First Two Decades of the Movement', Ph.D., Bedford College, University of London, 1961.

Smyth, Dorothy Pearl, 'The Playwrights of the Irish Literary Renaissance', M.A., Acadia University, 1936.

Suss, Irving David, 'The Decline and Fall of Irish Drama', Ph.D., Columbia University, 1951.

Thompson, William I., 'Easter 1916: A Study of Literature and Revolution', Ph.D., Cornell University, 1966.

Wickstrom, Gordon M., 'The Deirdre Plays of AE, Yeats, and Synge: Patterns of Irish Exile', Ph.D., Stanford University, 1969.

Worth, Katharine J., 'Symbolism in Modern English Drama', Ph.D., University of London, 1953.

2 SAMUEL BECKETT

*Dissertations dealing exclusively with
the fiction of Beckett are not included*

Abel, Adeline, 'Aspects de la Mort dans le Théâtre de Camus,
Tandieu, Ionesco, Genet et Beckett', Ph.D., Louisiana State
University, 1967.

Benjamin, Sybil, 'Tragicomic Catharsis in Samuel Beckett's
En Attendant Godot', Ph.D., Northern Illinois University,
1970.

Cohn, Ruby Haykin, 'Samuel Beckett; The Comic Gamut',
Ph.D., University of Washington, St Louis, 1960.

Frisch, Jack Eugene, 'Ironic Theatre: Techniques of Irony in
Plays of Samuel Beckett, Eugene Ionesco, Harold Pinter and
Jean Genet', Ph.D., University of Wisconsin, 1964.

Gatting, Charles J., 'Pirandello, *Umorismo*, and Beckett',
Ph.D., Southern Illinois University, 1967.

Gordon, Lois G., 'Dialectic of the Beast and the Monk: The
Dramatic Rhetoric of Samuel Beckett', Ph.D., University of
Wisconsin, 1966.

Hampton, Charles C., 'The Human Situation in the Plays of
Samuel Beckett: A Study of Stratagems of Inaction', Ph.D.,
Stanford University, 1966.

Hench, Michael M., 'The Use of Paradox as Artistic Technique
in Beckett's Plays', Ph.D., University of Massachusetts,
1969.

Juergens, Robert Oscar, 'Theatricality in the Avant-Garde: An

Objective Analysis of Selected Plays of Pinter, Beckett, and Ionesco', Ph.D., Yale University, 1968.

Metz, Mary Seawell, 'Existentialism and Inauthenticity in the Theatre of Beckett, Ionesco and Genet', Ph.D., Louisiana State University, 1966.

Radke, Judith Joy, 'Doubt and the Disintegration of Form in the French Novels and Drama of Samuel Beckett', Ph.D., University of Colorado, 1961.

Rogers, W. T., 'The Theatre of Ambiguity' [Beckett, Ionesco, Genet, Pinter], Ph.D., Florida State University, 1969.

Ross, Margaret, 'L'expression du temps dans l'oeuvre de Samuel Beckett', M.A., Dalhousie University, 1968.

Saigal, Prem K., 'Samuel Beckett's Theatre: An Existential Approach', M.A., University of Alberta, 1968.

Shartar, Martin I., 'The Theatre of Mind: Mallarmé, Yeats, Eliot and Beckett', Ph.D., Emory University, 1966.

Theroux, Alexander L., 'The Language of Samuel Beckett', Ph.D., University of Virginia, 1968.

Watson, Richard A., 'God Games: Some Explorations of the Theatrical Structures of Modern Narrative Literature: Beckett, Ionesco and Pinter', Ph.D., University of Washington, 1968.

Wells, C. Michael, 'The Transcendence of Life: the Positive Dimension in Samuel Beckett', Ph.D., University of New Mexico, 1968.

Yungblut, June J., 'The Morphology of the Impasse: A Study of Samuel Beckett's Work', Ph.D., Emory University, 1968.

3 DION BOUCICAULT

Anderson, Jesse M., 'Dion Boucicault; Man of the Theatre', Ph.D., University of Chicago, 1926.

Folland, Harold, 'The Plays of Dion Boucicault', Ph.D., Harvard University, 1940.

Orr, Lynn E., 'Dion Boucicault and the Nineteenth-Century Theatre', Ph.D., Louisiana State University, 1953.

Rohrig, Gladys M., 'An Analysis of Certain Acting Editions and Prompt Books of Plays of Dion Boucicault', Ph.D., Ohio State University, 1956.

Tolson, Julius H., 'Dion Boucicault', Ph.D., University of Pennsylvania, 1951.

McGuire, James Brady, 'Realism in Irish Drama', Ph.D., Trinity
  College Dublin, 1954.

5 LORD DUNSANY

La Croix, J. F., 'Lord Dunsany', Ph.D., Trinity College Dublin, 1956.

Haile, Virginia A., 'The Dramas and Dramatic Criticism of St John Greer Ervine', Ph.D., Indiana University, 1949.

Scofield, J. M., 'The Dramatic Work of Mr. St John Ervine', M.A., University of Wales, 1952.

7 GEORGE FITZMAURICE

McGuire, James Brady, 'Realism in Irish Drama', Ph.D., Trinity
College Dublin, 1954.

Balderston, Katherine Canby, 'The History and Sources of Percy's Memoir of Goldsmith', Ph.D., Yale University, 1925.

Bastian, John L., 'Smollett's and Goldsmith's Histories and the Mid-Eighteenth Century Reaction to the Genre of History', Ph.D., University of Boston, 1952.

Bell, Howard J., Jr., 'The Social Philosophy of Oliver Goldsmith', Ph.D., Princeton University, 1937.

Clarke, Kathleen O., 'Oliver Goldsmith as a Literary Critic', M.A., University College London, 1951.

Coulter, John Knox, 'Oliver Goldsmith's Literary Reputation, 1757-1801', Ph.D., Indiana University, 1965.

Fan, Twen-Chung, 'Chinese Culture in England from Sir William Temple to Oliver Goldsmith', Ph.D., Harvard University, 1931.

Friedman, Arthur, 'Studies in the Canon and Sources of Oliver Goldsmith', Ph.D., University of Chicago, 1938.

Goldenbroit, Morris, 'Internal Evidence and Goldsmith's Periodical Writings', Ph.D., New York University, 1953.

Griffin, Robert Julian, 'Goldsmith's Augustanism; A Study of His Literary Works', Ph.D., University of California, 1965.

Hopkins, Robert Hazen, 'The Creative Genius of Oliver Goldsmith', Ph.D., University of Pennsylvania, 1961.

Johnstone, Coragreene, 'The Literary Views of Oliver Goldsmith', Ph.D., University of Michigan, 1952.

Lowenstein, Amy, 'Annals of the Poor, Social Fact and Artistic Response in Gray, Goldsmith, Cowper, Crabbe, Blake, Burns', Ph.D., New York University, 1968.

Lynskey, Winnifred C., 'Goldsmith's Interest in Natural History, 1759-74', Ph.D., University of Chicago, 1941.

Macey, Samuel L., 'Theatrical Satire as a Reflection of Changing Tastes — Buckingham, Gay, Duffet, Fielding, Sheridan, and Goldsmith', Ph.D., University of Washington at Seattle, 1967.

Murphy, Elisabeth Ann, 'Goldsmith's Intellectual Background', Ph.D., University of Wisconsin, 1943.

Murphy, Sr Miriam J., 'A Revaluation of the Works of Oliver Goldsmith', Ph.D., University of Wisconsin, 1953.

Nelick, Franklyn C., 'Oliver Goldsmith: Traveller', Ph.D., University of Wisconsin, 1952.

Pitman, James Hall, 'Goldsmith's Animated Nature; A Study of Goldsmith', Ph.D., Yale University, 1922.

Tupper, Caroline Frances, 'Oliver Goldsmith as a Critic', Ph.D., Radcliffe University, 1917.

9 LADY GREGORY

Byars, John Arthur, 'The Heroic Type in the Irish Legendary Dramas of W. B. Yeats, Lady Gregory, and J. M. Synge, 1903-1910', Ph.D., University of North Carolina, 1963.

Donovan, D. C., 'Lady Gregory and the Abbey Theatre', M.A., National University of Ireland, Dublin, 1950.

McGuire, James Brady, 'Realism in Irish Drama', Ph.D., Trinity College Dublin, 1954.

Murphy, Daniel, 'The Letters of Lady Gregory to John Quinn', Ph.D., University of Columbia, 1962.

Regan, M. J., 'Lady Gregory; the Dramatic Artist', M.A., National University of Ireland, Dublin, 1952.

Young, L. D., 'The Plays of Lady Gregory', Ph.D., Trinity College Dublin, 1957.

Ferrar, Harold, 'Denis Johnston and the Irish Theatre', Ph.D.,
Columbia University, 1968.

West, F. W., 'The Life and Works of Denis Johnston', Ph.D.,
University of Leeds, 1967.

11 JAMES JOYCE

Dissertations dealing exclusively with the
novels of Joyce are not included in this section

Gullette, David G., 'Linguistic Dualism in the Works of James Joyce', Ph.D., University of North Carolina, 1968.

Lameyer, Gordon A., 'The Automystic and the Cultic Twalette: Spiritual and Spiritualistic Concerns in the Works of James Joyce', Ph.D., Columbia University, 1969.

McElhaney, James H., 'The Irish Cyclist. An Inquiry into the Theme of Death and Rebirth in James Joyce', Ph.D., Pennsylvania State University, 1966.

O'Brien, Darcy G., 'The Conscience of James Joyce', Ph.D., University of California at Berkeley, 1966.

Solomon, Albert J., 'James Joyce and George Moore: A Study of a Literary Relationship', Ph.D., Pennsylvania State, 1969.

Staley, Harry C., 'James Joyce and the Catechism', Ph.D., Pennsylvania University, 1967.

Swinson, Henry W., 'Joyce and the Theatre', Ph.D., University of Illinois, 1969.

Hazard, Forrest Earl, 'The Auden Group and the Group
   Theatre; The Dramatic Theories and Practices of Rupert
   Doone, W. H. Auden, Christopher Isherwood, Louis
   MacNeice, Stephen Spender, and Cecil Day Lewis', Ph.D.,
   University of Wisconsin, 1964.

McGuire, James Brady, 'Realism in Irish Drama', Ph.D., Trinity College Dublin, 1954.

Harris, John B., 'Charles Robert Maturin: A Study', Ph.D., Wayne State University, 1966.

Armato, Philip M., 'Theory and Practice in George Moore's Major Drama, 1897-1930', Ph.D., Purdue University, 1970.

Brown, Malcolm J., 'George Moore's Criticism', Ph.D., University of Washington at Seattle, 1947.

Kennedy, Sr Eileen, 'Circling Back: The Influence of Ireland on George Moore', Ph.D., Columbia University, 1968.

McGuire, James Brady, 'Realism in Irish Drama', Ph.D., Trinity College Dublin, 1954.

Sinfelt, Frederick W., 'The Unconventional Realism of George Moore', Ph.D., Pennsylvania State University, 1967.

Small, Ray, 'A Critical Edition of Diarmuid and Grania, by William Butler Yeats and George Moore', Ph.D., University of Texas, 1958.

Stock, J. C., 'The Role of Conscience in the Early Works of George Moore', M.Litt., Trinity College Dublin, 1967.

Weaver, Jack W., 'A Story-teller's Holiday: George Moore's Irish Renaissance, 1897-1911', Ph.D., University of North Carolina, 1966.

Conlin, E. T., 'T. C. Murray; A Critical Study of His Dramatic Work', Ph.D., National University of Ireland, Dublin, 1952.

Allt, G. D. P., 'The Anglo-Irish Literary Movement in Relation to Its Antecedents', Ph.D., Cambridge University, 1952.

Ayling, Ronald, 'The Dramatic Artistry of Sean O'Casey: A Study of Theme and Form in the Plays Written for the Abbey Theatre, 1922-1928', Ph.D., University of Bristol, 1968.

Bernardbehan, Brother Merrill, 'Anglo-Irish Literature', M.A., University of Montreal, 1939.

Buckley, Ian, 'An Analysis of the Plays of Sean O'Casey', M.A., University of Kent at Canterbury, 1970.

Caswell, Robert W., 'Sean O'Casey as a Poetic Dramatist', Ph.D., Trinity College Dublin, 1960.

Cole, A. S., 'Stagecraft in the Modern Dublin Theatre', Ph.D., Trinity College Dublin, 1953.

Cooper, Mabel, 'The Irish Theatre: Its History and Its Dramatists', M.A., University of Manitoba, 1931.

Coston, Herbert Hull, 'The Idea of Courage in the Works of Sean O'Casey', Ph.D., Columbia University, 1960.

Cowasjee, Saros, 'Sean O'Casey: The Man Behind the Plays', Ph.D., University of Leeds, 1959.

Daniel, Walter C., 'O'Casey and the Comic', Ph.D., Bowling Green University, 1963.

Darin, Davis, 'Influences on the Dramas of Sean O'Casey', Ph.D., New York University, 1969.

Esslinger, Patricia Moore, 'The Dublin *Materia Poetica* of Sean O'Casey', Ph.D., Tulane University, 1960.

Firth, John Mirkil, 'O'Casey and Autobiography', Ph.D., University of Virginia, 1965.

Garrison, Emery Clayton, 'The Structure of Sean O'Casey's Plays', Ph.D., Stanford University, 1956.

Hogan, Robert, 'Sean O'Casey's Experiments in Dramatic Form', Ph.D., University of Missouri, 1956.

Howse, Hans Frederick, 'The Plays of Sean O'Casey', M.A., University of Liverpool, 1951.

Krause, David, 'Prometheus of Dublin; A Study of the Plays of Sean O'Casey', Ph.D., New York University, 1956.

Kregosky, Joanne Irene, 'O'Casey's Autobiographies and Their Relationship to His Drama', M.A., University of Alberta, 1968.

Landow, Ursula Trask, 'O'Casey and His Critics as Seen Through the Nathan Correspondence', M.A., Cornell University, 1961.

Larson, Gerald A., 'The Dramaturgy of Sean O'Casey', Ph.D., University of Utah, 1957.

Locklin, Mae, 'Sean O'Casey: A Critical Study', M.A., Queen's University, Kingston, 1932.

McGuire, James Brady, 'Realism in Irish Drama', Ph.D., Trinity College Dublin, 1954.

Maitra, Lila, 'Sean O'Casey; A Critical Review', Ph.D., University of Calcutta, 1960.

Malone, M. G., 'The Plays of Sean O'Casey in Relation to Their Political and Social Background', M.A., King's College, University of London, 1964.

Maroldo, William John, 'Sean O'Casey and the Art of Autobiography: Form and Content in the Irish Books', Ph.D., Columbia University, 1964.

Massey, Jack, 'The Development of the Theme in the Plays of Sean O'Casey, with a Study of Some Technical Devices Common to His Plays', M.A., Birkbeck College, University of London, 1955.

Metscher, Thomas, 'Sean O'Casey's Dramatischer Stil', Ph.D., Heidelberg University, 1967.

Moya, Carmela, 'L'Univers de Sean O'Casey', Ph.D., University of Paris, 1969.

Nordell, Hans Roderick, 'The Dramatic Practice and Theory of Sean O'Casey', B.Litt., Trinity College Dublin, 1951.

O'Neill, Michael J., 'The Diaries of a Dublin Playgoer as a Mirror of the Irish Literary Revival', Ph.D., National University, Dublin, 1952.

O'Riley, Margaret Catherine, 'The Dramaturgy of Sean O'Casey', Ph.D., University of Wisconsin, 1955.

Palter, Lewis, 'The Comedy in the Plays of Sean O'Casey', Ph.D., Northwestern University, 1965.

Peteler, Patricia M., 'The Social and Symbolic Drama of the English-Language Theatre, 1929-1949', Ph.D., University of Utah, 1961.

Pixley, Edward E., 'A Structural Analysis of Eight of Sean O'Casey's Plays', Ph.D., University of Iowa, 1969.

Poggemiller, Marion D., 'Sean O'Casey's Last Plays: A Collection of Life', M.A., University of British Columbia, 1968.

Ritchie, Harry M., 'Form and Content in the Plays of Sean O'Casey', D.F.A., Yale University, 1960.

Rollins, Ronald Gene, 'Sean O'Casey: The Man with Two Faces', Ph.D., University of Cincinnati, 1960.

Saddlemyer, E. Ann, 'A Study of the Dramatic Theory Developed by the Founders of the Irish Literary Theatre and the Attempt to Apply This Theory in the Abbey Theatre, with Particular Reference to the Achievements of the Major Figures during the First Two Decades of the Movement', Ph.D., Bedford College, University of London, 1961.

Schrank, Bernice S., 'Reflection of Reality: A Study in the Uses of Language and Time in the Plays of Sean O'Casey', Ph.D., University of Wisconsin, 1969.

Smith, Bobby L., 'Satire in the Drama of Sean O'Casey', Ph.D., University of Oklahoma, 1965.

Smyth, Dorothy Pearl, 'The Playwrights of the Irish Literary Renaissance', M.A., Acadia University, 1936.

Suss, Irving David, 'The Decline and Fall of Irish Drama', Ph.D., Columbia University, 1951.

Templeton, Alice Joan, 'Expressionism in British and American Drama', Ph.D., University of Oregon, 1966.

Thomas, Noel K., 'The Major Plays of Sean O'Casey Considered in the Light of Their Theatrical Production and Critical Reception', Ph.D., University of Birmingham, 1963.

Williamson, Ward, 'An Analytical History of American Criticism of the Works of Sean O'Casey, 1924-1958', Ph.D., State University of Iowa, 1962.

Wittig, Kurt, 'Sean O'Casey Als Dramatiker. Ein Beitrag Zum Nachkriegsdrama Irlands', Ph.D., Halle University, 1937.

Worth, Katharine J., 'Symbolism in Modern English Drama', Ph.D., University of London, 1953.

McGuire, James Brady, 'Realism in Irish Drama', Ph.D., Trinity College Dublin, 1954.

Smith, C. B., 'Unity in Diversity: A Critical Study of the Drama of Lennox Robinson', Ph.D., Trinity College Dublin, 1960.

Merchant, Francis J., 'The Place of AE in Irish Culture', Ph.D., New York University, 1952.

Wickstrom, Gordon M., 'The Deirdre Plays of AE, Yeats, and Synge: Patterns of Irish Exile', Ph.D., Stanford University, 1969.

Abbott, Anthony Sternsen, 'Shaw and Christianity', Ph.D., Harvard University, 1962.

Adams, Elsie B., 'Bernard Shaw and the Aesthetes', Ph.D., University of Oklahoma, 1966.

Alt, Edward O., 'Shaw Und Der Fabianismus', Ph.D., Freiburg University, 1956.

Al-Wakil, A. W. A. R., 'The Themes and Methods of Bernard Shaw as a Dramatist of Ideas, with a Critical Assessment of His Achievement', M.A., University of Manchester, 1957.

Anders, Margarete, 'Die Historischen Komoedien von George Bernard Shaw', Ph.D., Heidelberg University, 1921.

Austin, Don Deforest, 'The Comic Structure in Five Plays of Bernard Shaw', Ph.D., University of Washington, 1960.

Baake, Friedrich, 'George Bernard Shaw Als Musikschriftsteller', Ph.D., Kiel University, 1953.

Bader, Earl D., 'The Self-Reflective Language: Uses of Paradox in Wilde, Shaw and Chesterton', Ph.D., Indiana University, 1969.

Barber, George S., 'The Musical Criticism of Bernard Shaw', Ph.D., Pennsylvania State University, 1953.

Barr, Alan Philip, 'Bernard Shaw as a Religious Dramatist', Ph.D., Rochester University, 1963.

Bennett, Kenneth Chrisholm, Jr, 'George Bernard Shaw's Philosophy of Art', Ph.D., Indiana University, 1962.

Bernd, Daniel Walter, 'The Dramatic Theory of George Bernard Shaw', Ph.D., University of Nebraska, 1962.

Berst, Charles Ashton, 'Bernard Shaw's Comic Perspective; A View of Self and Reality', Ph.D., University of Washington, 1965.

Besant, Lloyd Alfred, 'Shaw's Women Characters', Ph.D., University of Wisconsin, 1964.

Besenbruch, Max L., 'Shaw Als Historiker', Ph.D., Erlangen University, 1951.

Bhakri, A. S. N., 'Shaw's Dramas in Relation to His Social and Philosophical Ideas', Ph.D., University of Leeds, 1956.

Bhatia, H. L., 'Shaw the Dramatist: A Class by Himself', M.A., University of Liverpool, 1967.

Bond, George Robert, 'The Method of Iconoclasm in George Bernard Shaw', Ph.D., University of Michigan, 1959.

Bowman, David H., 'Bernard Shaw's *Three Plays for Puritans*', Ph.D., University of Chicago, 1969.

Boxhill, Roger E., 'Shaw and the Doctors', Ph.D., Columbia University, 1966.

Bringle, Jerald E., 'The First Unpleasant Play by Bernard Shaw: An Analysis of the Formation and Evolution of *Widowers' Houses*', Ph.D., New York University, 1969.

Byers, William F., 'The Nineteenth Century English Farce and Its Influence on Bernard Shaw', Ph.D., Columbia University, 1963.

Carpenter, Charles Albert, 'Bernard Shaw's Development as a

Dramatic Artist, 1884-1899', Ph.D., Cornell University, 1963.

Cathey, Kenneth Clay, 'George Bernard Shaw's Drama of Ideas', Ph.D., University of Vanderbilt, 1958

Cirillo, Nancy R., 'The Poet Aimed: Wagner, D'Annunzio, Shaw', Ph.D., New York University, 1968.

Clayton, Robert Bovee, 'The Salvation Myth in the Drama of George Bernard Shaw', Ph.D., University of California, 1961.

Cohn, Erna, 'Eltern Und Kinder Bei Bernard Shaw', Ph.D., Leipzig University, 1927.

Costello, Donald P., 'George Bernard Shaw and the Motion Picture; His Theory and Practice', Ph.D., University of Chicago, 1962.

Crane, Gladys, 'The Characterization of the Comic Women Characters of George Bernard Shaw', Ph.D., Indiana University, 1968.

Dietrich, Richard F., 'The Emerging Superman; A Study of Shaw's Novels', Ph.D., Florida State University at Tallahassee, 1965.

Doering, Anneliese, 'Untersuchungen Zu Bernard Shaws The Perfect Wagnerite', Ph.D., Giessen University, 1945.

Donaghy, Henry J., 'A Comparison of the Thought of George Bernard Shaw and G. K. Chesterton', Ph.D., New York University, 1966.

Dower, Margaret Winifred, 'The Political and Social Thinking of George Bernard Shaw', Ph.D., Boston University, 1957.

Dupler, Dorothy, 'An Analytical Study of the Use of Rhetorical Devices in Three Selected Plays of George

Bernard Shaw', Ph.D., University of Southern California, 1961.

Ebel, Walter, 'Das Geschlechterproblem Bei Bernhard Shaw', Ph.D., Koenigsberg University, 1925.

England, A. W., 'Action and Argument in the Plays of Bernard Shaw's Middle Period', M.A., University of Liverpool, 1967.

Er-Rai, A., 'The Shavian Drama: Influence on the Technique', University of Birmingham, 1955.

Fischer, Friedrich, 'George Bernard Shaw Als Dramatiker Und Sein Verhaeltnis Zu Henrik Ibsen', Ph.D., Münster University, 1917.

Fordyce, William D. T., 'Bernard Shaw and the Comedy of Medicine: A Study of *The Doctor's Dilemma*', Ph.D., Harvard University, 1967.

Forter, Elizabeth T., 'A Study of the Dramatic Technique of Bernard Shaw', Ph.D., University of Wisconsin, 1955.

Frazer, Frances, 'An Edition of *Three Plays for Puritans*', Ph.D., Birkbeck College, University of London, 1969.

Fromm, Harold, 'Bernard Shaw and the Theaters of the Nineties', Ph.D., University of Wisconsin, 1962.

Furlong, William Benedict, 'The Shaw-Chesterton Literary Relationship', Ph.D., Pennsylvania State University, 1968.

Geduld, Harry M., 'An Edition of *Back to Methuselah*', Ph.D., Birkbeck College, University of London, 1962.

Gerould, Daniel Charles, 'The Critical Reception of Shaw's Plays in France, 1908-1950', Ph.D., University of Chicago, 1960.

Gillespie, Charles Richard, 'A Study of Characterization in

Selected Disquisitory Plays of Bernard Shaw', Ph.D., University of Iowa, 1961.

Goodykoontz, William Francis, 'John Bunyan's Influence on George Bernard Shaw', Ph.D., University of North Carolina, 1956.

Gowman, H. D., 'Bernard Shaw's Theory and Practice of Dramatic Presentation', M.A., University of Wales, 1956.

Graham, Philip Bruce, 'Bernard Shaw's Dramatic Technique, 1892-1924', Ph.D., Yale University, 1960.

Groshong, James Willard, 'G. B. S. (George Bernard Shaw) and Germany; The Major Aspects', Ph.D., Stanford University, 1957.

Hales, John, 'Shaw's Comedy', Ph.D., University of Texas, 1963.

Hatcher, Joe B., 'G. B. S. on the Minor Dramatists of the Nineties', Ph.D., University of Kansas, 1968.

Herrin, Virginia T., 'Bernard Shaw and Richard Wagner; A Study of Their Intellectual Kinship as Artist Philosophers', Ph.D., University of North Carolina, 1955.

Heuser, Hilde, 'Die Eigenart Des Sozialismus George Bernard Shaw', Ph.D., Frankfurt University, 1934.

Hoeffinghoff, Gerda, 'George Bernard Shaw Als Publizist', Ph.D., Münster University, 1950.

Holt, Charles Lloyd, 'The Musical Dramaturgy of Bernard Shaw', Ph.D., Wayne State University, 1963.

Hornby, Richard, 'Bernard Shaw's Dark Comedies', Ph.D., Tulane University, 1967.

Hubenka, Lloyd J., 'The Religious Philosophy of Bernard Shaw', Ph.D., University of Nebraska, 1966.

Hummert, Paul A., 'Marxist Elements in the Works of George Bernard Shaw', Ph.D., Northwestern University, 1953.

Hutchinson, P. William, 'A Comparative Study of the Professional Religionist as a Character in the Plays of George Bernard Shaw', Ph.D., Northwestern University, 1968.

Jago, D. M., 'Tradition and Progress in Shaw and Wells, Belloc and Chesterton', Ph.D., University of Leicester, 1965.

Karr, Harold S., 'Samuel Butler: His Influence on Shaw, Forster and Lawrence', Ph.D., University of Minnesota, 1953.

Kaye, Julian B., 'Bernard Shaw and the Nineteenth Century Tradition', Ph.D., Columbia University, 1954.

Kemelman, A. F., 'The Influence of Samuel Butler on George Bernard Shaw', M.A., University of Liverpool, 1967.

Keough, Lawrence C., 'The Critical Reception of the Major Plays of George Bernard Shaw Performed in New York, 1894-1950', Ph.D., University of Southern California, 1969.

Kinyon, F. John, 'Bernard Shaw and the Irish Question', Ph.D., University of Nebraska, 1969.

Knepper, Bill G., '*Back to Methuselah* and the Utopian Tradition', Ph.D., University of Nebraska, 1967.

Kutzsch, Gerhard, 'Der Fall *Candida*. Eine Kritische Untersuchung Ueber George Bernard Shaw Als Problemdramatiker Und Seine Wirkung', Ph.D., Leipzig University, 1941.

Lapan, Maureen Therese, 'An Analysis of Selected Plays of Bernard Shaw as Media for the Examination of "Closed

Areas" of Contemporary Society by Secondary School Students', Ed.D., University of Connecticut, 1962.

Larson, Gale K., 'Bernard Shaw's *Caesar and Cleopatra* as History', Ph.D., University of Nebraska, 1968.

Leary, Daniel James, 'The Superman and Structure in George Bernard Shaw's Plays; A Study in Dialectic Action', Ph.D., University of Syracuse, 1958.

Lehmann, Wilhelm, 'George Bernard Shaws Verhaeltnis Zu Romantik Und Idealismus', Ph.D., Bonn University, 1934.

Lengnick, Paul, 'Ehe Und Famile Bei Bernard Shaw', Ph.D., Königsberg University, 1933.

Lorenz, Rolf, 'Bernard Shaws Aiseinandersetzung Mit Der Tragik Des Daseins', Ph.D., Hamburg University, 1937.

Lynch, Vernon E., 'George Bernard Shaw and the Comic', Ph.D., University of Texas, 1951.

McCague, Wilma Gallagher, 'The Influence of Shaw's Experience as a Director of Plays on His Stage Directions', Ph.D., Ohio State University, 1937.

Mai, Werner, 'Das Drama George Bernard Shaws Auf Der Deutschen Buehne Und In Der Deutschen Kritik', Ph.D., Tübingen University, 1954.

Manson, Donald D., 'Bernard Shaw's Use of Wit in Selected Speeches', Ph.D., Pennsylvania State University, 1967.

Mason, M.A., 'The Early Plays of Bernard Shaw, up to 1910, in Relation to the Social Background and Ideas of the Time', Ph.D., King's College, University of London, 1965.

Meisel, Martin, 'Shaw and the Nineteenth Century Theatre', Ph.D., Princeton University, 1960.

Metwally, A. A., 'The Influences of Ibsen on Shaw', Ph.D., Trinity College Dublin, 1960.

Mills, Carl Henry, 'The Intellectual and Literary Background of George Bernard Shaw's *Man and Superman*', Ph.D., University of Nebraska, 1965.

Mills, John Arvin, 'Language and Laughter; A Study of Comic Diction in the Plays of Bernard Shaw', Ph.D., Indiana University, 1962.

Munitz, Barry, 'Joan of Arc and Modern Drama', Ph.D., Princeton University, 1968.

Nelson, Raymond S., 'Religion and the Plays of George Bernard Shaw', Ph.D., University of Nebraska, 1968.

Nickson, Joseph Richard, 'The Art and Politics of the Later Plays of Bernard Shaw', Ph.D., University of Southern California, 1958.

Nicolaysen, Lorenz, 'Untersuchungen Über Bernard Shaw', Ph.D., Hamburg University, 1923.

O'Bolger, Thomas Denis, 'George Bernard Shaw's Social Philosophy', Ph.D., University of Pennsylvania, 1913.

Ohmann, Richard Malin, 'Studies in Prose Style: Arnold, Shaw, Wilde', Ph.D., Harvard University, 1960.

Paxon, Omar M., 'Bernard Shaw's Stage Directions', Ph.D., Northwestern University, 1961.

Peper, Elisabeth, 'George Bernard Shaws Beziehungen Zu Samuel Butler Dem Juengeren', Ph.D., Königsberg University, 1927.

Pettet, Edwin Burr, 'Shavian Socialism and the Shavian Life Force; An Analysis of the Relationship between the Philosophic and Economic Systems of George Bernard Shaw', Ph.D., New York University, 1951.

Philipp, Guenther B., 'Bernard Shaws Stellung Zu Demokratie Und Faschismus', Ph.D., Münster University, 1950.

Pierce, Glenn Quimby, 'Arnold Daly's Productions of Plays by Bernard Shaw', Ph.D., University of Illinois, 1961.

Pilecki, Gerard Anthony, 'Shaw's Geneva: A Critical Study of the Evolution of the Text in Relation to Shaw's Political Thought and Dramatic Practice', Ph.D., Cornell University, 1961.

Pilger, Else, 'George Bernard Shaw in Deutschland', Ph.D., Münster University, 1942.

Pitt, D. K., 'Tragic Perspectives with Particular Reference to the Plays of Bernard Shaw and Arthur Miller', M.A., University of Liverpool, 1967.

Plotinsky, Melvin Lloyd, 'The Play of the Mind; A Study of Bernard Shaw's Dramatic Apprenticeship', Ph.D., Harvard University, 1963.

Regan, Arthur E., 'Farce and Fantasy in Bernard Shaw', Ph.D., Harvard University, 1965.

Rehback, Wilhelm, 'George Bernard Shaw Als Dramatiker', Ph.D., Erlangen University, 1915.

Reuben, Elaine, 'The Social Dramatist: A Study of Shaw's English Family Plays', Ph.D., Stanford University, 1970.

Robinson, M. E., 'Verse and Prose in Modern British Drama: A Study of the Literary Forms Developed by Four Representative Playwrights—Shaw, Synge, Yeats and T. S. Eliot', M.A., University of Manchester, 1957.

Rogers, Richard E., 'Didacticism, Plot and Comedy: Ways in Which George Bernard Shaw Uses Plot to Keep Comic His Didactic Purpose', Ph.D., Indiana University, 1969.

Salesbury, Rita-Lynne, 'The Theme of Conversion and Salvation in the Plays of Bernard Shaw', M.A., University of Saskatchewan, 1966.

Schindler, Gerhard, 'Shaws Kritik Am English Way of Life', Ph.D., Leipzig University, 1954.

Scott, Robert Lee, 'Bernard Shaw's Rhetorical Drama; A Study of Rhetoric and Poetic in Selected Plays', Ph.D., University of Illinois, 1956.

Searle, William M., 'The Saint and the Skeptics: Joan of Arc in the Works of Mark Twain, Anatole France and Bernard Shaw', Ph.D., University of California at Berkeley, 1968.

Seidel, Christian, 'Die Entwicklung Eines Fabiers, George Bernard Shaw', Ph.D., München University, 1962.

Sharp, William L., 'The Relation of Dramatic Structure to the Comedy in the Plays of George Bernard Shaw', Ph.D., Stanford University, 1954.

Shields, Jean Louise, 'Shaw's Women Characters; An Analysis and a Survey of Influences from His Life', University of Indiana, 1959.

Simon, Louis, 'The Educational Theories of George Bernard Shaw', Ph.D., New York University, 1956.

Smith, Robert M., 'Modern Dramatic Censorship; George Bernard Shaw', Ph.D., University of Indiana, 1954.

Soerensen, Edith D., 'G. B. Shaws Puritanismus', Ph.D., Hamburg University, 1940.

Soucie, Robert M., 'Dramatic Theory and Practice in G. B. Shaw: *Our Theatres in the Nineties* and the Plays to *Caesar and Cleopatra*', M.A., University of Toronto, 1966.

Speckhard, Robert Reidel, 'Shaw and Aristophanes; A Study

of the Eiron, Agon, Alazon, Doctor/Cook and Sacred Marriage in Shavian Comedy', Ph.D., University of Michigan, 1959.

Spector, Samuel Hardy, 'The Social and Educational Philosophy of George Bernard Shaw', Ed.D., Wayne State University, 1958.

Spencer, Terence James, 'The Dramatic Principles of George Bernard Shaw', Ph.D., Stanford University, 1957.

Stockholder, Fred Edward, Jr, 'G. B. Shaw's German Philosophy of History and the Significant Form of His Plays', Ph.D., University of Washington, 1964.

Stokes, Elmore E., Jr, 'William Morris and Bernard Shaw; A Socialist-Artistic Relationship', Ph.D., University of Texas, 1951.

Stoppel, Hans, 'Das Bild Menschlicher Groesse Bei Bernard Shaw', Ph.D., Kiel University, 1950.

Stow, Glenys Mary, 'Bernard Shaw as a Poetic Dramatist', M.A., McMaster University, 1967.

Talley, Jerry B., 'Religious Themes in the Dramatic Works of George Bernard Shaw, T. S. Eliot, and Paul Claudel', Ph.D., University of Denver, 1964.

Timmler, Markus, 'Die Anschauungen Bernard Shaws Über Die Aufgaben Des Theaters Auf Grund Seiner Theorie und Praxis', Ph.D., Königsberg University, 1936.

Tyson, Brian F., 'The Evolution of G. B. Shaw's *Plays Unpleasant*', Ph.D., University College London, 1968.

Veilleux, Jere Shanor, 'An Analysis of the Rhetorical Situation and Rhetorical Character Types in Selected Plays of George Bernard Shaw', Ph.D., University of Minnesota, 1957.

Wall, Vincent C., Jr, 'Shaw the Statesman', Ph.D., University of Wisconsin, 1938.

Watson, Barbara B., 'A Shavian Guide to the Intelligent Woman', Ph.D., Columbia University, 1963.

Whalen, J. P., 'Some Structural Similarities in John Bunyan's *The Pilgrim's Progress* and Selected Narrative and Dramatic Work of George Bernard Shaw', Ph.D., University of Pittsburgh, 1968.

White, Jean Westrum, 'Shaw on the New York Stage', Ph.D., New York University, 1966.

Williams, Jeffrey A., 'Theme and Structure in Bernard Shaw's Political Plays of the 1930s', M.A., University of British Columbia, 1968.

Wilson, E. Edwin, Jr, 'Shaw's Shakespearean Criticism', D.F.A., Yale University, 1958.

Zeller, Hermann, 'Die Frauengestalten In Bernard Shaws Dramatischen Werken', Ph.D., Tübingen University, 1936.

Zerke, Carl F., 'George Bernard Shaw's Ideas on Acting', Ph.D., Florida State University, 1954.

Cook, William E., 'Sheridan's Comedy of Deception', Ph.D., Harvard University, 1967.

Hartmann, Hermann, 'Über Die Vorlagen Zu Sheridans Rivals', Ph.D., Königsberg University, 1888.

Macey, Samuel L., 'Theatrical Satire as a Reflection of Changing Tastes – Buckingham, Gat, Duffet, Fielding, Sheridan, and Goldsmith', Ph.D., University of Washington at Seattle, 1967.

Niederduer, George R., Rev., 'Wit and Sentiment in Sheridan's Comedies of Manners', Ph.D., University of Southern California, 1966.

Oliver, Robert T., 'A Re-Evaluation of the Oratory of Burke, Fox, Sheridan, and Pitt', Ph.D., University of Wisconsin, 1937.

Purdy, Richard Little, 'The Rivals, A Comedy; As It Was First Acted at the Theatre-Royal in Covent Garden. Written by Richard Brinsley Sheridan, Esq. Edited from the Larpent MS', Ph.D., Yale University, 1930.

Sawyer, Newell Wheeler, 'The Comedy of Manners from Sheridan to Maugham. A Study of the Type as a Dramatic Form and as a Social Document', Ph.D., University of Pennsylvania, 1930.

Steuber, Fritz, 'Sheridans Rivals. Entstehungsgeschichte Und Beitraege Zu Einer Deutschen Theatergeschichte Des Stueckes', Ph.D., Marburg University, 1913.

Taylor, Garland F., 'Richard Brinsley Sheridan's *The Duenna*', Ph.D., Yale University, 1940.

Wadlington, Mary Emme (Mrs Herbert A. Barnes), 'Mrs Frances Sheridan; Her Life and Works. Including A Study of Her Influence on R. B. Sheridan's Plays, and an Edition of Her Comedy, *The Discovery*', Ph.D., Yale University, 1914.

Walker, Fred B., 'A Rhetorical Study of the Parliamentary Speaking of Richard Brinsley Sheridan on the Rights of Ireland', Ph.D., George Peabody University, 1968.

Weiss, Kurt, 'Richard Brinsley Sheridan Als Lustspieldichter', Ph.D., Leipzig University, 1888.

Kelly, J. J., 'George Shiels as the Exponent of Modern Irish Comedy', M.A., National University of Ireland, Dublin, 1950.

Abood, Edward F., 'The Reception of the Abbey Theater in America, 1911-14', Ph.D., University of Chicago, 1963.

Allt, G. D. P., 'The Anglo-Irish Literary Movement in Relation to Its Antecedents', Ph.D., Cambridge University, 1952.

Aufhauser, Annemarie, 'Sind Die Dremen Von John Millington Synge Durch Franzqesische Vorbilder Beeinflusst', Ph.D., München University, 1935.

Brady, M., 'John Millington Synge, the Dramatic Artist', M.A., National University of Ireland, Dublin, 1952.

Carmody, Terence F., 'John Millington Synge: A Study of the Intruder in His Wicklow Plays', M.Litt., Trinity College Dublin, 1963.

Bernardbehan, Brother Merrill, 'Anglo-Irish Literature', M.A., University of Montreal, 1939.

Berrow, J. H., 'A Study of the Background Treatment and Presentation of Irish Character in British Plays from the Late 19th Century to the Present Day', M.A., University of Wales, Swansea, 1966.

Byars, John Arthur, 'The Heroic Type in the Irish Legendary Dramas of W. B. Yeats, Lady Gregory, and J. M. Synge: 1903-1910', Ph.D., University of North Carolina, Chapel Hill, 1963.

Cole, A. S., 'Stagecraft in the Modern Dublin Theatre', Ph.D., Trinity College, Dublin, 1953.

Coleman, Sr Anne G., 'Social and Political Satire in Irish Drama', Ph.D., University of Fordham, 1954.

Cooper, Mabel, 'The Irish Theatre: Its History and Its Dramatists', M.A., University of Manitoba, 1931.

Cotter, Eileen Mary, 'The Deirdre Theme in Anglo-Irish Literature', Ph.D., University of California, Los Angeles, 1966.

Estill, Adelaide Duncan, 'The Sources of Synge', Ph.D., University of Pennsylvania, 1937 [published].

Flood, Jeanne Agnes, 'John Millington Synge; A Study of His Aesthetic Development', Ph.D., University of Michigan, 1967.

Frese, J. J., 'The Coalescence of Theme and Language in the Comedies of J. M. Synge', M.Litt., Trinity College Dublin, 1961.

Frenzel, Herbert, 'John Millington Synge's Work as a Contribution to Irish Folk-Lore and to the Psychology of Primitive Tribes', Ph.D., University of Bonn, 1932 [published].

Fulbeck, John Frederick, 'A Comparative Study of Poetic Elements in Selected Plays by John Millington Synge and by Frederico Garcia Lorca', Ph.D., University of Southern California, 1960.

Greene, David Herbert, 'The Drama of J. M. Synge; A Critical Study', Ph.D., Harvard University, 1944.

Hillery, J., 'John Millington Synge: A Study of the Dramatic Structure of His Tragedies', M.Litt., Trinity College Dublin, 1960.

Jennings, Michael, 'Synge's Selective World-View', M.A., Ohio Wesleyan University, 1969.

Kelson, John Hofstad, 'Nationalism in the Theater: The Ole Bull Theater in Norway and the Abbey Theater in Ireland: A Comparative Study', Ph.D., University of Kansas, 1964.

Kilroy, James Francis, 'Dominant Themes and Ironic Techniques in the Works of J. M. Synge', Ph.D., University of Wisconsin, 1965.

Kostandi, F. M. G., 'A Reconsideration of H. A. Jones, Pinero, Wilde, Synge, with Special Reference to the Influence of Ibsen', Ph.D., Manchester University, 1964.

Krieger, Hans, 'John Millington Synge, ein dichter der "keltischen renaissance"', Ph.D., Marburg University, 1916 [published].

Lyman, Kenneth C., 'Critical Reaction to Irish Drama on the New York Stage, 1900-1958', Ph.D., University of Wisconsin, 1960.

McGuire, James Brady, 'Realism in Irish Drama', Ph.D., Trinity College Dublin, 1954.

McKinley, C. F., 'John Millington Synge', Ph.D., Trinity College Dublin, 1951.

Miller, Marcia S. K., 'The Deirdre Legend in English Literature', Ph.D., University of Pennsylvania, 1950.

Newlin, Nicholas, 'The Language of Synge's Plays; The Irish Element', Ph.D., University of Pennsylvania, 1949.

O'Neill, Michael J., 'The Diaries of a Dublin Playgoer as a Mirror of the Irish Literary Revival', Ph.D., National University, Dublin, 1952.

Osborn, Margaret Elizabeth, 'The Concept of Imagination in Edwardian Drama', Ph.D., Pennsylvania State University, 1967.

Peteler, Patricia M., 'The Social and Symbolic Drama of the English-Language Theatre, 1929-1949', Ph.D., University of Utah, 1961.

Price, A. F., 'The Art of John M. Synge', M.A., University of Liverpool, 1951.

Randall, Ethel Claire, 'The Celtic Movement: The Awakening of the Fires', M.A., University of Chicago, 1906.

Robinson, M. E., 'Verse and Prose in Modern British Drama: A Study of the Literary Forms Developed by Four Representative Playwrights—Shaw, Synge, Yeats and T. S. Eliot', M.A., University of Manchester, 1957.

Saddlemyer, E. Ann, 'A Study of the Dramatic Theory Developed by the Founders of the Irish Literary Theatre and the Attempt to Apply This Theory in the Abbey Theatre, with Particular Reference to the Achievement of the Major Figures during the First Two Decades of the Movement', Ph.D., Bedford College, University of London, 1961.

Smoot, Amelia Jean Johannessen, 'A Comparison of Plays by John Millington Synge and Frederico Garcia Lorca: The Poets and Time', Ph.D., University of North Carolina, Chapel Hill, 1967.

Smyth, Dorothy Pearl, 'The Playwrights of the Irish Literary Renaissance', M.A., Acadia University, 1936.

Sorg, J. L., 'Synge and Shakespeare: A Comparison of Approaches to Tragi-Comedy', B.Litt., Trinity College Dublin, 1954.

Suss, Irving David, 'The Decline and Fall of Irish Drama', Ph.D., Columbia University, 1951.

Takacs, Dalma S., 'J. M. Synge as a Dramatist', Ph.D., Columbia University, 1969.

Turner, David Michael, 'Word Patterns in the Drama of John Millington Synge', M.A., University of Manitoba, 1967.

Wickstrom, Gordon M., 'The Deirdre Plays of AE, Yeats, and Synge: Patterns of Irish Exile', Ph.D., Stanford University, 1969.

Worth, Katharine J., 'Symbolism in Modern English Drama', Ph.D., University of London, 1953.

Alexander, Beverly G., 'Oscar Wilde's Plays on the New York Stage, 1882-1950', M.A., Columbia University, 1951.

Anderson, Lorine, 'A Century of Dandyism, from Poe and Baudelaire to Wallace Stevens', M.A., Columbia University, 1954.

Berland, Ellen, 'Form and Content in the Plays of Oscar Wilde', Ph.D., Columbia University, 1969.

Bock, Edward J., 'Walter Paters Einfluss Auf Oscar Wilde', Ph.D., Bonn University, 1913.

Bronte, Diana, 'The Influence of Oscar Wilde in the Life and Prose Fiction of Andre Gidé', Ph.D., University of North Carolina at Chapel Hill, 1969.

Cubbon, W. M., 'Development and Significance of Oscar Wilde's Theory of Art', M.A., University of Manchester, 1947.

Dudley, Leonea Barbour, 'The Language of Comedy; An Introductory Analysis of the Verbal Forms of the Comic Spirit in Drama', Ph.D., Cornell University, 1945.

Ganz, Arthur F., 'The Dandiacal Drama; A Study of the Plays of Oscar Wilde, Ph.D., Columbia University, 1957.

Gulley, Paul M., 'Philosophical Consistency in the Works of Oscar Wilde', Ph.D., University of Oklahoma, 1967.

Hardman, Dorothy Johnson, 'Oscar Wilde's Plays on the New York Professional Stage', M.A., University of Washington, 1942.

James, Norman, 'Oscar Wilde's Dramaturgy', Ph.D., Duke University, 1959.

Kaufman, Esther, 'The Use of Oriental Material by James Thomson, Oscar Wilde, and Rudyard Kipling', Ph.D., Cornell University, 1948.

Kostandi, F. M. G., 'A Reconsideration of H. A. Jones, Pinero, Wilde, Synge, with Special Reference to the Influence of Ibsen', Ph.D., University of Manchester, 1964.

Lord, J. K., 'The Comedies of Oscar Wilde: A General Semantic Interpretation', Ph.D., New York University, 1970.

Mikhail, E. H., 'The Comedies of Oscar Wilde; A Critique. Together with a Comprehensive Bibliography', Ph.D., University of Sheffield, 1966.

O'Brien, Kevin, 'Oscar Wilde and the Maritimes', M.A., University of New Brunswick, 1967.

Ohmann, Richard Malin, 'Studies in Prose Style: Arnold, Shaw, Wilde', Ph.D., Harvard University, 1960.

Poteet, Lewis J., 'Romantic Aesthetics in Oscar Wilde's Prose', Ph.D., University of Minnesota, 1968.

Rhodes, Robert Edward, 'The Literary Criticism of Oscar Wilde', Ph.D., University of Michigan, 1964.

Recoulley, Alfred L., 'Oscar Wilde, the Dandy-Artist. A Study of Dandyism in the Life and Works of Oscar Wilde, with Particular Attention to the Intellectual Bases of Wilde's Dandyism', Ph.D., University of North Carolina, 1968.

Stanton, Stephen Sadler, 'English Drama and the French Well-Made Play, 1815-1915', Ph.D., Columbia University, 1955.

Wadleigh, Paul Custer, 'Form in Oscar Wilde's Comedies; A Structural Analysis', Ph.D., Indiana University, 1962.

Wong, Helene Har Lin, 'The Late Victorian Theatre as Reflected in *The Theatre* 1878-1897', Ph.D., Louisiana State University, 1955.

Allen, James Lovic, Jr, 'Bird Symbolism in the Work of William Butler Yeats', Ph.D. University of Florida, 1959.

Allt, G. D. P., 'The Anglo-Irish Literary Movement in Relation to Its Antecedents', Ph.D., Cambridge University, 1952.

Archibald, Douglas N., 'W. B. Yeats' Encounters with Swift, Berkeley, and Burke', Ph.D., University of Michigan, 1966.

Babu, M. Sathya, 'Christian Themes and Symbols in the Later Poetry of W. B. Yeats', Ph.D., University of Wisconsin, 1968.

Bachchan, H. R., 'W. B. Yeats and Occultism: A Study of His Works in Relation to Indian Lore, the Cabbala, Swedenborg, Böhme and Theosophy', Ph.D., Cambridge University, 1954.

Baksi, P., 'Yeats and Eliot as Theorists of Contemporary Drama; A Comparative Study', M.A., Birkbeck College, University of London, 1966.

Becker, A. W. J., 'The Work of W. B. Yeats in the Field of Drama', D.Phil., Oxford University, 1953.

Benson, Carl F., ' A Study of Yeats' *A Vision*', Ph.D., University of Illinois, 1948.

Bernardbehan, Brother Merrill, 'Anglo-Irish Literature', M.A., University of Montreal, 1939.

Berryman, Charles B., 'W. B. Yeats; Design of Opposites', Ph.D., University of Wisconsin, 1965.

Berwind, Sandra M., 'The Origins of a Poet; A Study of the Critical Prose of W. B. Yeats, 1887-1907', Ph.D., Bryn Mawr University, 1968.

Blau, Herbert, 'William Butler Yeats and Thomas Stearns Eliot; Poetic Drama and Modern Poetry', Ph.D., Stanford University, 1954.

Bornstein, George J., 'The Surfeited Alastor; William Butler Yeats' Changing Relation to Percy Bysshe Shelley', Ph.D., Princeton University, 1966.

Brawn, John T., 'The Apostrophic Gesture', Ph.D., University of Washington at Seattle, 1967.

Broder, Peggy Fisher, 'Positive Folly: the Role of the Fool in the Works of W. B. Yeats', Ph.D., Case Western Reserve University, 1969.

Brueggemann, Theodor, 'Das Christliche Element in William Butler Yeats Dichterischer Symbolik', Ph.D., Münster University, 1955.

Burghardt, Larraine, 'Modern Criticism and the Drama of W. B. Yeats', Ph.D., University of Chicago, 1968.

Bushrui, S. B., 'Yeats Revision of His Verse-Plays, 1900-1910', Ph.D., University of Southampton, 1962.

Byars, John Arthur, 'The Heroic Type in the Irish Legendary Dramas of W. B. Yeats, Lady Gregory, and J. M. Synge, 1903-1910', Ph.D., University of North Carolina, 1963.

Byrd, Thomas L., Jr, 'The Early Poetry of W. B. Yeats, The Poetic Quest', Ph.D., University of Florida at Gainsville, 1968.

Clark, David R., 'W. B. Yeats' Development as a Dramatist', Ph.D., Yale University, 1955.

Colwell, Frederic S., 'W. B. Yeats – the Dimensions of Poetic Vision', Michigan State University, 1966.

Conner, Lester I., 'A Yeats Dictionary; Names of the Persons and Places in the Poetry of W. B. Yeats', Ph.D., Columbia University, 1964.

Cooper, Mabel, 'The Irish Theatre; Its History and Its Dramatists', M.A., University of Manitoba, 1931.

Cooper, Philip, Jr, 'Lyric Ambivalence; An Essay on the Poetry of William Butler Yeats and Robert Lowell', Ph.D., Rochester University, 1967.

Copeland, Tom W., 'The Proper Names in William Butler Yeats' Non-Dramatic Poetry', Ph.D., Texas Technical University, 1957.

Cotter, Eileen M., 'The Deirdre Theme in Anglo-Irish Literature', Ph.D., University of California, 1967.

Dasgupta, Pranabendu, 'The "Subjective" Tradition; A Comparative Analysis of the Dramatic Motives in the Plays of W. B. Yeats and Rabindranath Tagore', Ph.D., University of Minnesota, 1966.

Davis, Dorothy R., 'Parallelism between Classical Tragedy and the Tragedy of William Butler Yeats', Ph.D., University of Boston, 1937.

Davis, E., 'A Study of Affinities between W. B. Yeats and French Symbolists', B.Litt., Oxford University, 1954.

Davis, Robert B., 'The Shaping of an Agate; A Study of the Development of the Literary Theory of W. B. Yeats from 1885 to 1910', Ph.D., University of Chicago, 1956.

Denton, Marilyn J., 'The Form of Yeats' Lyric Poetry', Ph.D., University of Wisconsin, 1957.

Desai, Rupina, 'Yeats and Shakespeare', Ph.D., Northwestern University, 1968.

Donaldson, A. R., 'The Influence of Irish Nationalism upon the Early Development of W. B. Yeats', M.A., Queen Mary College, University of London, 1953.

Donohue, D., 'A Study of Modern English Verse Drama', Ph.D., National University of Ireland, Dublin, 1957.

Dume, Thomas L., 'William Butler Yeats; A Study of His Reading', Ph.D., Temple University, 1950.

Eddins, Dwight L., 'Yeats: the Nineteenth Century Matrix', Ph.D., Vanderbilt University, 1967.

Egerer, Sr Mary Anne Monica, 'The Rogueries of William Butler Yeats', Ph.D., Radcliffe University, 1962.

Ellmann, Richard D., 'Triton among the Streams; A Study of the Life and Writings of William Butler Yeats', Ph.D., Yale University, 1947.

Engleberg, Edward, 'The Herald of Art; A Study of W. B. Yeats' Criticism and Aesthetic', Ph.D., University of Wisconsin, 1958.

Farag, F. F., 'Oriental Mysticism in W. B. Yeats', Ph.D., University of Edinburgh, 1960.

Faulk, Carolyn S., 'The Apollonian and Dionysian Modes in Lyric Poetry and Their Development in the Poetry of W. B. Yeats and Dylan Thomas', Ph.D., University of Illinois, 1963.

Finneran, Richard J., 'A Critical Edition of William Butler Yeats' *John Sherman and Dhoya*', Ph.D., University of North Carolina, 1968.

Fite, Monte D., 'Yeats as an Editor of Blake; Interpretation and Emendation in the Works of William Blake, Poetic, Symbolic, and Critical', Ph.D., University of North Carolina, 1968.

Franklin, Laura M., 'The Development of Yeats' Poetic Diction', Ph.D., Northwestern University, 1956.

Frayne, John P., 'The Early Critical Prose of W. B. Yeats; Forty-One Reviews, Edited, with an Introduction and Notes', Ph.D., Columbia University, 1967.

Garab, Arra M., 'Beyond Byzantium; Studies in the Later Poetry of William Butler Yeats', Ph.D., Columbia University, 1963.

Goldman, Michael Paul, 'The Point of Drama; The Concept of Reverie in the Plays of William Butler Yeats', Ph.D., Princeton University, 1962.

Goodman, Henry, 'The Plays of William Butler Yeats as Myth and Ritual', Ph.D., University of Minnesota, 1953.

Gowda, H. H. A., 'English Verse Drama from 1890-1935', M.Litt., University of Durham, 1959.

Grab, Frederic Daniel, 'William Butler Yeats and Greek Literature', Ph.D., University of California, 1965.

Green, Howard L., 'The Poetry of W. B. Yeats; A Critical Evaluation', Ph.D., Stanford University, 1953.

Grill, Richard, 'Der Junge Yeats und Der Franzoesische Symbolismus', Ph.D., Freiburg University, 1952.

Grossman, Allen R., 'The Last Judgment of the Imagination; a Study of Yeats' *The Wind among the Reeds*', Ph.D., Brandeis University, 1960.

Guha, Naresh, 'W. B. Yeats; An Indian View', Ph.D., Northwestern University, 1962.

Hahn, Sr M. Norma, 'Yeats' Search for Reality; A Study of the Imagery of His Later Poetry', Ph.D., Fordham University, 1960.

Hassan, Ihab H., 'French Symbolism and Modern British Poetry, with Yeats, Eliot and Edith Sitwell as Indices', Ph.D., University of Pennsylvania, 1953.

Hethmon, Robert Henry, Jr, 'The Theatre's Anti-Self; A Study of the Symbolism of Yeats' Unpopular Plays', Ph.D., Stanford University, 1957.

Hollis, James R., 'Patterns of Opposition and Reconciliation in the Life and Work of W. B. Yeats', Ph.D., Drew University, 1967.

Hood, Walter K., 'A Study of *A Vision* by W. B. Yeats', Ph.D., University of North Carolina, 1968.

Horsley, L. S., 'Song and Fatherland—W. B. Yeats and the Tradition of Thomas Davis, 1886-1905', Ph.D., University of Reading, 1966.

Hubert, Claire M., 'The Still Point and the Turning World; A Comparison of the Myths of Gerard de Nerval and William Butler Yeats', Ph.D., Emory University, 1965.

Huettemann, Gerta, 'Wesen Der Dichtung Und Aufgabe Dichters Bei William Butler Yeats', Ph.D., University of Bonn, 1929.

Jacquet, Katherine, 'Greek Aspects of W. B. Yeats's Plays of the Irish Heroic Age', Ph.D., Arizona State University, 1967.

Jameson, Grace E., 'Mysticism in A.E. and Yeats in Relation to Oriental and American Thought', Ph.D., Ohio State University, 1932.

Jeffares, A. N., 'W. B. Yeats, Man and Poet', D.Phil., Oxford University, 1947.

Jochum, Klaus-Peter, 'Die Dramatische Struktur der Spiele von W. B. Yeats', Ph.D., Frankfurt University, 1968.

John, B., 'The Philosophical Ideas of W. B. Yeats', M.A., University of Wales, 1958.

Johnson, Colton, 'W. B. Yeats's Prose Contributions to Periodicals, 1900-1939', Ph.D., Northwestern University, 1968.

Jones, David R., 'The Poet in the Theatre', Ph.D., Princeton University, 1968.

Keep, William C., 'Yeats and the Public', Ph.D., University of Washington, 1965.

Kehoe, C. de, 'The Tradition of the Irish Poet in the Work of William Butler Yeats', Ph.D., Trinity College Dublin, 1967.

Kersnowski, Frank Louis, Jr, 'The Irish Scene in Yeats's Drama', Ph.D., University of Kansas, 1963.

Khan, S. W., 'Indian Elements in the Works of Yeats, Eliot, and Huxley', Ph.D., University of Nottingham, 1956.

Kim, Myung Whan, 'Mythopoetic Elements in the Later Plays of W. B. Yeats and the Noh', Ph.D., Indiana University, 1969.

Klimek, Theodor, 'Symbol und Wirklichkeit Untersuchungen Zu William Butler Yeats Poetischer Theoric', Ph.D., University of Hamburg, 1967.

Komesu, Ohifumi, 'W. B. Yeats; Vision and Experience', Ph.D., Michigan State University, 1968.

Lederman, Marie Jean, 'The Myth of the Dead and Resurrected God in Seven Plays of W. B. Yeats: A Psychoanalytic Interpretation', Ph.D., New York University, 1966.

Levine, Bernard, 'The Dissolving Image; A Concentrative Analysis of Yeats' Poetry', Ph.D., Brown University, 1965.

Linebarger, James Morris, 'Yeats' Symbolist Method and the Play *Purgatory*', Ph.D., Emory University, 1963.

Mahon, C. M., 'The Fascination of What's Difficult: W. B. Yeats, the Mask as Disciple and Esthetic', Ph.D., University of California at Santa Barbara. 1967.

Manvell, A. R., 'The Study of W. B. Yeats's Poetic Career with Special Reference to His Lyrical Poems', Ph.D., University of London, 1938.

Merritt, Robert Gray, 'Euripides and Yeats; The Parallel Progression of Their Plays', Ph.D., Tulane University, 1963.

Miller, Marcia S. K., 'The Deirdre Legend in English Literature', Ph.D., University of Pennsylvania, 1950.

Mobridge, John D., 'Primal and Bardic; The Role of Ireland in Yeats' Early Aesthetics', University of Illinois, 1967.

Mohr, Martin Alfred, 'The Political and Social Thought of William Butler Yeats', Ph.D., University of Iowa, 1964.

Moore, John Rees, 'Evolution of Myth in the Plays of W. B. Yeats', Ph.D., Columbia University, 1957.

Moore, Virginia, 'Religion and William Butler Yeats', Ph.D., Columbia University, 1952.

Morgan, J. M., 'W. B. Yeats: A Study of the Symbolic Patterns Found in His Later Poems and Plays', B.Litt., Oxford University, 1953.

Nathan, Edward Leonard, 'W. B. Yeats' Development as a Tragic Dramatist, 1884-1939', Ph.D., University of California, 1961.

O'Brien, James H., 'Theosophy and the Poetry of George

Russell, William Butler Yeats, and James Stephens', Ph.D., University of Washington at Seattle, 1956.

O'Connell, Adelyn, 'A Study of Rhythmic Structure in the Verse of William Butler Yeats', Ph.D., Catholic University, 1966.

O'Grady, Anne F., 'Yeats's Ancestral Theatre', M.A., University of Alberta, 1967.

O'Neill, Michael J., 'The Diaries of a Dublin Playgoer as a Mirror of the Irish Literary Revival', Ph.D., National University, Dublin, 1952.

Parker, J. S., 'The Modern Poet as Dramatist: Some Aspects of Non-Realistic Drama, with Special Reference to Eliot, Yeats and Cummings', M.A., The Queen's University, Belfast, 1966.

Parkinson, Thomas F., 'Yeats as Critic of His Early Verse', Ph.D., University of California at Berkeley, 1949.

Parks, Lloyd Clifford, 'The Influence of Villiers de l'Isle-Adam on W. B. Yeats', Ph.D., University of Washington, 1960.

Pearce, Donald R., 'The Significance of Ireland in the Work of W. B. Yeats', Ph.D., University of Michigan, 1949.

Peteler, Patricia M., 'The Social and Symbolic Drama of the English-Language Theatre, 1929-1949', Ph.D., University of Utah, 1961.

Poletta, Gregory, 'The Progress in W. B. Yeats' Theories of Poetry', Ph.D., Princeton University, 1961.

Prosky, Murray D., 'Landscapes in the Poetry of W. B. Yeats', Ph.D., University of Wisconsin, 1966.

Rasmussen, Audrey L., 'The Drama of William Butler Yeats', Ph.D., University of Wisconsin, 1953.

Reaney, James, 'The Influence of Spencer on Yeats', Ph.D., University of Toronto, 1958.

Reeves, Herbert A., 'The Dramatic Effectiveness of Yeats's Imagery in the Later Plays', Ph.D., Stanford University, 1968.

Reid, Benjamin Lawrence, 'W. B. Yeats and Generic Tragedy', Ph.D., University of Virginia, 1957.

Reischle, Helmut, 'Die Sieben Fassungen Des Dramas *The Countess Cathleen* von W. B. Yeats. Ein Vergleich', Ph.D., Tübingen University, 1961.

Richman, Larry Kermit, 'The Theme of Self-Sacrifice in Yeats' Drama', Ph.D., Duke University, 1969.

Robinson, M. E., 'Verse and Prose in Modern British Drama: A Study of Literary Forms Developed by Four Representative Playwrights – Shaw, Synge, Yeats and T. S. Eliot', M.A., University of Manchester, 1957.

Ronsley, Joseph, 'The Design of the Autobiography of W. B. Yeats', Ph.D., Northwestern University, 1966.

Rose, Phyllis Hoge, 'Yeats and the Dramatic Lyric', Ph.D., University of Wisconsin, 1958.

Rothfuss, Heinrich, 'Wandlungen in Der Spacten Lyrik William Butler Yeats', Ph.D., Tübingen University, 1966.

Ruthledge, Robert C., 'The Development of the Poetry of William Butler Yeats as Reflected in His Metaphors', Ph.D., George Washington University, 1966.

Ryan, Sr M. Rosalie, 'Symbolic Elements in the Plays of W. B. Yeats, 1891-1921', Ph.D., Catholic University, 1953.

Saddlemyer, E. A., 'A Study of the Dramatic Theory Developed by the Founders of the Irish Literary Theatre and the

Attempt to Apply This Theory in the Abbey Theatre, with Particular Reference to the Achievement of the Major Figures during the First Two Decades of the Movement', Ph.D., Bedford College, University of London, 1961.

Saha, Prosanta Kumar, 'Yeats's Cuchulain Works: Some Aspects of Style and Thematic Development', Ph.D., Western Reserve University, 1966.

Sanborn, C. E., 'W. B. Yeats: His Views of History', Ph.D., University of Toronto, 1959.

Schmalenbeck, Hildegard, 'The Early Career of W. B. Yeats', Ph.D., University of Texas, 1957.

Schmitt, Natalie Sue, 'The Ritual of a Lost Faith: the Drama of William Butler Yeats', Ph.D., Stanford University, 1968.

Schweisgut, Elsbeth, 'Yeats Feendichtung', Ph.D., Giessen University, 1927.

Seiden, Morton I., 'William Butler Yeats; His Poetry and His Vision — 1914-1939', Ph.D., Columbia University, 1952.

Seyppel, Jeannette L., 'William Butler Yeats, Die Bildersprache Seiner Lyrik', Ph.D., University of Berlin, 1966.

Shartar, Martin I., 'The Theatre of Mind: Mallarmé, Yeats, Eliot and Beckett', Ph.D., Emory University, 1966.

Shaw, Priscilla W., 'The Conception of the Self in Rilke, Valéry, and Yeats', Ph.D., Yale University, 1960.

Sidnell, Michael J., 'A Critical Examination of W. B. Yeats's *The Shadowy Waters*, with a Transcription and Collation of the Manuscript Versions', Ph.D., External College, University of London, 1967.

Skene, Reginald R., 'The Unity of the Cuchulain Cycle of Plays by W. B. Yeats', M.A., University of Manitoba, 1967.

Small, Ray, 'A Critical Edition of Diarmuid and Grania, by William Butler Yeats and George Moore', Ph.D., University of Texas, 1958.

Smith, Ellen R., 'Yeats's Cultural Touchstone: the Period from Dante to Shakespeare', Ph.D., University of Michigan, 1968.

Smyth, Dorothy Pearl, 'The Playwrights of the Irish Literary Renaissance', M.A., Acadia University, 1936.

Spivak, Gayatri C., 'The Great Wheel; Stages in the Personality of Yeats' Lyric Speaker', Ph.D., Cornell University, 1967.

Stead, C. K., 'The New Poetic; An Investigation into Certain Common Problems Evident in the Work of English-Speaking Poets of the Twentieth Century, the Study Confined Mainly to the Literary Scene in England from 1900 to 1930, and Paying Special Attention to the Work of W. B. Yeats and T. S. Eliot', Ph.D., University of Bristol, 1961.

Stewart, R., 'Those Masterful Images; A Study of Yeats' Symbols of Unity and Joy as Aspects of Romanticism', Ph.D., Yale University, 1968.

Strabel, Audrey L. E., 'Yeats' Development of a Symbolic Drama', Ph.D., University of Wisconsin, 1953.

Sullivan, John J., 'The Great Design; Yeats' Rearrangement of His Poems', Ph.D., University of Virginia, 1966.

Suss, Irving David, 'The Decline and Fall of Irish Drama', Ph.D., Columbia University, 1951.

Torchiana, Donald Thornhill, 'W. B. Yeats' Literary Use of Certain Anglo-Irish Augustans', Ph.D., University of Iowa, 1953.

Tsukimura, Reiko, 'The Language of Symbolism in Yeats and Hagiwara', Ph.D., Indiana University, 1967.

Tutiah, Marvis, 'The Relations between Music and Poetry in the Plays of Shakespeare and Yeats, with Particular Reference to *Twelfth Night* and *At the Hawk's Well*', M.A., University of Manitoba, 1967.

Unterecker, John Eugene, 'A Study of the Function of Bird and Tree Imagery in the Works of W. B. Yeats', Ph.D., Columbia University, 1956.

Vanderhaar, Margaret M., 'Yeats' Relationships with Women and Their Influence on His Poetry', Ph.D., University of Tulane, 1966.

Vendler, Helen Marie Hennessy, 'A Study of W. B. Yeats's Vision and the Plays Related to It', Ph.D., Radcliffe University, 1960.

Verhulst, Margaret M., 'Myth and Symbol in the Plays of W. B. Yeats', Ph.D., University of Texas at Austin, 1969.

Warschausky, Sidney, 'W. B. Yeats as Literary Critic', Ph.D., Columbia University, 1957.

Watson, Thomas L., 'A Critical Edition of Selected Lyrics of William Butler Yeats', Ph.D., University of Texas, 1958.

Webster, Brenda Ann, 'The Dream and the Dreamer in the Works of W. B. Yeats', Ph.D., University of California at Berkeley, 1967.

West, William Channing, 'Concepts of Reality in the Poetic Drama of W. B. Yeats, W. H. Auden, and T. S. Eliot', Ph.D., Stanford University, 1964.

Whitaker, Thomas R., 'W. B. Yeats and His Concept of History', Ph.D., Yale University, 1953.

White, H., 'A Study of W. B. Yeats as a Dramatist, with Special Reference to His Treatment of the Ideas Formulated in "A Vision"', M.A., University of Leeds, 1956.

Wickstrom, Gordon M., 'The Deirdre Plays of AE, Yeats, and Synge: Patterns of Irish Exile', Ph.D., Stanford University, 1969.

Wiedner, Elsie Margaret, 'The Use of the Theatre for the Presentation of Metaphysical Ideas; A Comparative Study of William Butler Yeats and Paul Claudel', Ph.D., Radcliffe University, 1961.

Wiegner, Kathleen Knapp, 'W. B. Yeats and the Ritual Imagination', Ph.D., University of Wisconsin, 1967.

Wilson, F. A. C. C., 'W. B. Yeats: The Last Plays', Ph.D., Cambridge University, 1959.

Worth, Katharine J., 'Symbolism in Modern English Drama', Ph.D., University of London, 1953.

Youngblood, Sarah Helen, 'William Butler Yeats; The Mature Style', Ph.D., University of Oklahoma, 1958.

Zwerdling, Alex., 'Yeats and Heroic Ideal', Ph.D., Princeton University, 1960.

INDEX OF AUTHORS OF DISSERTATIONS

INDEX OF INSTITUTIONS

Index of Institutions